hunger

thirst

nourish

hunger

thirst

nourish

poems

elle michelle

wild
hair
PUBLISHING

for stephen
my better half of chocolate cake
for sophia, claire and graham
my semi-sweet morsels

Published by Elle Michelle

ISBN: 9798714103018

Library of Congress Control Number: 2021908056

Photographs, cover and interior design by Elle Michelle

Edited by Tabitha Cervantes

wild
hair
PUBLISHING

i hope you have come
hungry and thirsty
so that you may leave
nourished

and a little bit

buzzed

hunger

thirst

nourish

hunger

I WELCOME
THE TUG OF
HUNGER

AT LEAST
SOMETHING IS

DRAGGING

ME

FORWARD

a woman's place

why was my mother always the last to have a seat
at the dinner table, the one that she set so neat
she was always the last to have a bite of the food
the clean-up, well, that was her job too

my brother and i witnessed this growing up
why was it never her time to speak up
when children see their mothers as only those who serve
how can we expect them to grow up and treat women as they
deserve

it's now our job to break the cycle
show our sons and daughters that women are vital
in this world and in this life, they are more than able
and should always have an equal seat at the dinner table

spread like butter

thin
so thin
trying to please
everyone
but yourself
to the point
that no one
can even
taste
that you are there

being eaten alive

they stick needles the size of straws
into your breast to take
biopsy
after biopsy
after biopsy
but the cores removed from your body
are not nearly as painful
as the nagging thought
in your mind
that you could have
cancer
if the cancer isn't eating at your breast
the thought just might

as i watch my dad
inject our thanksgiving turkey
over and
over and
over
with butter and herbs
it makes me sick
to think that we are celebrating with food
while you are being eaten alive from the inside
from cancer or its possibility

malignant

you ripened too early
cantaloupes you couldn't hide
marks on your shoulders
from the heavy weight
scars on your brain
from the heavier stares
as soon as you found the strength
to hold them well
you found out they were rotting
on the inside
just as quickly as they had bloomed
they were plucked off
a part of you
now a specimen in a container
when the pathologist
sliced through
did she see your
memories magnified
that small window of time
when you were
whole

fall apart

when i fall apart
i don't
break
in
half
i don't melt into a puddle
i don't nervously laugh

i fall apart
like a cookie
little
crumbs
everywhere
impossible
to put back together
and the cleanup is a
nightmare

dirty innocence

i wish i could go back
to when i was a girl
making mud pies
in the backyard
without a care about
toe hair
breasts
or stained jeans
just the joy
for the simple things like
turning dirt and water into
mud pie feasts

you sat and watched
as he spat mashed potatoes
across the table and onto my face
during thanksgiving dinner
you did nothing

you stared blankly as i told you
how he flashed me and
grabbed my ass when i was
alone in my bedroom
you did nothing

when he called me a
dumb
ugly
whore
you did nothing

when he held me
under water in the pool
just a little too long
i needed you to save me and
you did nothing

am i nothing

i'm not your play dough

i must be an
easy target
too soft
too forgiving
because your claws
sank into my pliable dough
forcing me to
form and
reform
into whatever shape
made
you
look best

loud bark

you are
peanut brittle
happy to dish out
salty insults
but one hit
to your
ego
and you
shatter

any questions

everyone walked on
eggshells
around him
will he torture the dog
will he twist your nipple
will he insult your boyfriend
no one
was brave enough
to stand up to him
except cocaine
the coke stood up to him
it scrambled his brain

oreo divorce

you twisted the outer pieces
and pulled us apart at the center
you broke our family in half
like we weren't permanent, just renters

then you fought and fought and fought
about who would get the filling
the money and the house
and the children you were killing

on the inside, their fillings
were slowly nibbled away
by the squabbling and yelling
it didn't matter how much money you paid

the attorneys to help pull
our oreo family apart
when you tore our family in half
you broke everybody's heart

ginger break

they crushed our
frosted gingerbread house
under their feet
like two toddlers
fighting over
who gets to eat the
gum drop path

elle michelle

the orange tree

when i was five, we planted a tree
my mom, dad, brother and me
so fragile and small, only a couple of feet
those were the days we were happy to meet

the tree grew taller year after year
nourished by the waste produced from fear
outside a home that on the inside was breaking
while the orange tree was growing, thriving and taking

nourishment from the ground up from the roots
my family was rotting, and pruning its shoots
eventually we all went our separate ways
but the orange tree thrived, happy to stay

as a reminder
of the good
memories
we had when
we were whole
a beacon
of hope that
sometimes
we need to break
in order to grow

even after 30 years
you let a grudge
feast
on your heart
filling
plates and
plates and
plates
with would be
moments and memories
only to scrape them off into
the garbage

what a waste

you
pass
down
generations of
food obsession and
force feeding
sides around the table
onto the plates of your
children
teaching them to eat
past
the point of fullness
ensuring the
food addiction gene
does not
die
alone
with you

can you please pass the gluttony

airtight

i have learned
to hold back my words
preserves in a jar
stored up for winter
sweet notions
savory rampages and
sour remarks
sitting on the shelf
suppressed
behind their lids
until the seals are
broken
with a loud
POP

too me

they said i was too skinny
so i munched and munched and munched
then i was too tall
so i hunched and hunched and hunched
next my hair was too frizzy
so I made it behave and behave and behave
still i was too hairy
so i shaved and shaved and shaved
then suddenly i realized as
i ate and ate and ate
that i wasn't the problem
it was their hate and hate and hate

i will starve my body
to fit into a dress
that i will wear once
but what i'm really starving
is the love for myself
that i need to wear every day

self-love has no size

break out

sometimes i feel like the world
wants me to fit into their mold

cranberry sauce in a can
born with perfect lines

around the waist
ready to be passed and sliced

augmentation

many times
i've thought
about
replacing my
pear-sized
breasts for
melons

that i would let
someone
cut into my fruit
and leave
bruises and
scars

just so you
would feel satisfied
while browsing
the produce aisle
is completely

bananas

i peel off my leg hair
i peel off my eyebrows
i peel off my skin
until i look blank
like a peeled potato
just so i can feel comfortable
peeling off my clothes
not for myself
but for someone else

i like potato skins

elle michelle

stripped down

i want someone
who will accept every imperfection
of my body
when i'm wearing nothing
but a whipped cream bikini

hunger thirst nourish

carcinogenic

fashion
wants to brand me

with perfect grill lines
until i'm charred

with the stitches
of conformity

escargot

snobby
snobby
snobby
all rolled up
in your shell
you're too
bougie
to realize
you're
drowning in
your own
garlicky hell

quick spun ramifications

your gossip
spread
a drop of water on
cotton candy
sweet wild fire
for a second
then dissolved
instantly
into regret for the

damage done

no spinning it back
to the way it was

blushing skies

nosy cotton candy skies
blushing from secret lovers' deeds they've spied
i wish i could reach out and take a wisp
and let the secrets pass right through my lips
slowly melting on my tongue
i would breathe the mysteries deep into my lungs
to be able to feel what the skies have spied
might be too overwhelming for my human mind
so i'll feed my mouth earthly doings
and dream of what intrusive skies will be viewing

elle michelle

i can't catch my breath

sometimes i feel
trapped

between

trick candles
as soon as i blow one out
another is lighting
right beside it

mother shucker

we were two
scallop shells
held together
by the strongest muscle
until it was
cut
by a crooked knife

mr. lazy love

don't let your love get lazy
all sprawled out on the couch
munching chips and drinking pop
burping all the effort out

don't let your love get lazy
waking up at noon
forgetting to say i love you
letting your heart become immune

don't let your love get lazy
piles of dirty dishes in the sink
remnants of all your bad decisions
like my name on your chest in ink

don't let your love get lazy
clear vases now covered in spots
reminders of the flowers you'd buy me
now just wilted, dying thoughts

for when love gets lazy
you'll soon find yourself alone
spilling your regrets and sorrows
all over love's gravestone

and round
    and round
       and round
          we go as
            a lazy susan
              on the table
                meant to make everyone idle
                like our love
              we stay because it's easy
            we cycle between
        happiness
      boredom
    anger and
  indifference
caught in an endless loop of

going nowhere

the day that taste dies

i hope our taste buds for life
never grow so dull
that we need to cover everything in
gravy

cold dinners

you're hiding something
because you never skip dessert
you're playing with your potatoes
behind your eyes i see hurt

i wish you would tell me
i could help make it stop
we could enjoy a nice dinner
eat it while it's hot

but i know that won't happen
talking about it means you're weak
we'll let the hurt consume this moment
and eat cold dinners again this week

apron

i wear you
when he's in that mood
so that you will catch the debris
i don't want it to stain my white jeans
i don't want to have explain what's happening
between us
the wreckage
that's why i turn and smile
and tie you around my waist
this fight may take a while

love is easy
savory and sweet
silky and soft
every day a treat

love is simple
smooth and whole
comforting and calm
soothing to the soul

love is not forced
or won like a race
love should be natural
not an

acquired taste

the more i love you
the more i want to consume you
the more i consume you
the less of you there is

conserve love

save room

i have a bad habit of
overeating our love
leaving no room
for dessert

i'm the main course

you want me to be your garnish
sitting pretty on your plate
a parsley on your arm
when we go on fancy dates

there's no use for the garnish
she's always tossed aside
for the steak or the chicken
the dessert or the side

i want to be the sirloin
to your skillet pork chop
equal partners on the dish
anything else will be
the garnish on top

banana peel

protect my sweetness
from the pests that try to steal
my fruit all too soon

elle michelle

i'm not a switch

you can't turn me on like a microwave
heated up in a matter of seconds

i need to be slow cooked for hours
only then, will i

fall

to

pieces

midnight snacks

my body is not an open door
the fridge at midnight
spreading open at will for you

allowing you to take whatever snacks you desire
while a spotlight shines on the center of your face
illuminating your selfish hunger

wax(ed) lips

why do you act
like a kid in a candy shop
when i'm bare
down there
hairless
unnatural
like a kid
when you are an adult
acting like a kid
in a candy shop
and i am an adult
encouraging you
i think it's time we
act our age

elle michelle

sweet talk

don't sugar coat your words
i'll take them unsweetened
natural and raw

i never had a sweet tooth anyway

elle michelle

you're a spiny lobster

just because you
have a hard shell
doesn't mean
you are brave
every time i get
close
you retreat
backward
into a net of
loneliness

hunger thirst nourish

inside out poison

why do you crave the love of a maniac
who beats you up from the inside
chasing that sliver of light you once had
to make up for the thousands of times you have died

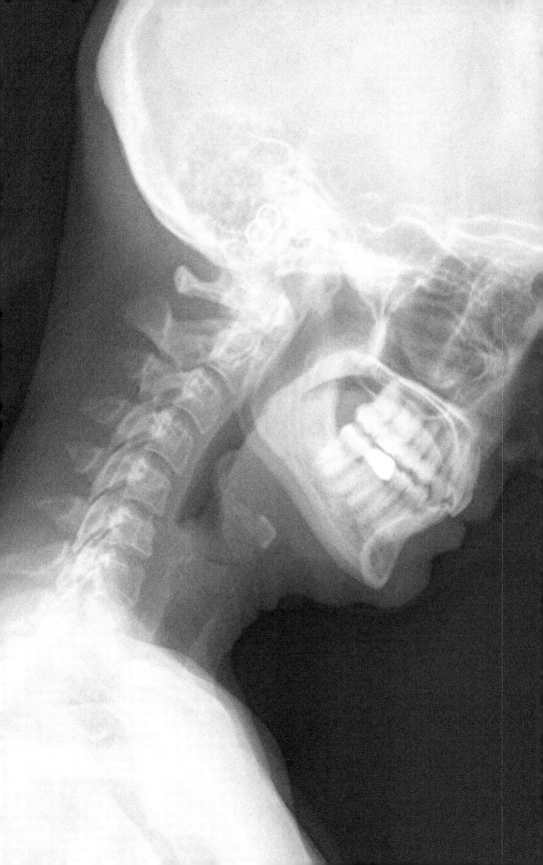

the char that broke my back

you held me under
the broiler
at first
it felt
warm
thrilling and
good
but I
can only take
so much
smoldering heat
before I start

to burn

why i stayed

the safe cradle
of a spoon
doesn't feel normal
after dancing
on the edge
of a knife

i started to feel
comfortable
with your sharp lines

knowing that
i would be
cut
but craving the
excitement
of not knowing

when

chocolate cloak

i wish i could cover our love in magic shell
keep it frozen forever
instantly hardened into place
chocolatey and sweet
until the first unknowing spoon
cracks into it
and shatters the magic

for the love of food

your mother fed you milk and cookies
instead of feeding you love
which taught you
to feed your dopamine receptors
with food
not love

why am i surprised then
when you pile your plate
only to throw it all up
so you can eat more

because you only feel love
when you eat food

and i'm not food

burnt popcorn

you always burned the bag
you didn't listen closely
to the slow of the pops
and the smell of the roasting

when you pop a bag for her
take a deep breath and let
the smell of the burn
be a lingering regret

elle michelle

i need to cut out your carbs

even when you left
i continued to make toast and honey
every morning
just the way you liked it
hoping that the smell
would somehow call you back to me

hunger thirst nourish

when you left

i shattered the jar of sprinkles on the floor
because you shattered
all the little pieces of happiness
inside my heart

sprinkles of the joy we had
now scattered on the kitchen floor

and every once in a while
i find one when i'm cleaning
sprinkled reminders of you
that will always be stuck to

the floorboards of my soul

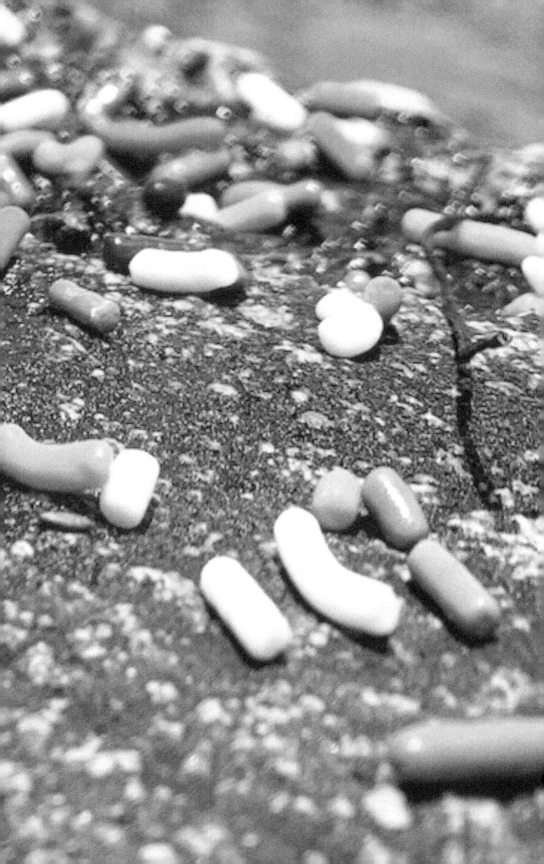

bad egg

i'm a hard-boiled egg
stiff and frozen in place
i wish you could dye me bright colors
and draw a smile back on my face

you scooped out
the piece of heart that
felt
the part I thought would
never
ever
m
 e
  l
   t

you left my heart out on the counter

you consumed
my heart like
the last donut
in the break room
taking
piece
by piece
by piece
until there was only
a stale sliver left
that no one
would touch

i should have put my name on it

THIRST
CAN LEAD YOU
TO THE PUNCH BOWL
BUT YOU HAVE TO DECIDE
IF YOU ARE GOING TO

S
P
I
K
E

IT

one sided

i tried to hold on to you
water cupped in my hands
always trying to slip
between my fingers

you wouldn't even hand me a glass

the corrosion of us

you tried to cut me
but i am water
i always come back together

you tried to spread me thin
but i am water
my internal bonds will stretch but not give

you tried to poke holes in me
slice me
stab me
and pierce me
but i am water

and you
are nothing but
a knife
that is now
rusted

narcissist

you stared into
your golden chalice
mesmerized by
your reflection
consumed so fully
by yourself
that you took a sip
of the poisoned liquid
you
yourself
had poured

elle michelle

macerated martyr

i let them stomp on me
like I was nothing
like i meant nothing
until all that was left was my skin
my insides squeezed out
grape juice to be fermented
so they could get drunk
on my essence

elle michelle

phantom love

it's like you're in a fog
your love is drunk on gin
going through the motions
of this life we're living in

your love used to be sober
you used to be so much fun
now you're here but not present
we might as well be done

so please walk out the door
or better yet float
on your drunk love vapors
to me you're like a
ghost

fizzled out love

our love is champagne
that's been left in the fridge
sour and flat
it's lost all its fizz

purgatory smells like espresso

you know that moment
in the morning
in between asleep and awake
that is the moment
that i smell you brewing espresso
just briefly
before i am startled awake
and i realize
that you are still gone
it was only a ghost
an apparition
haunting me
never passing to the other side
so that i may never fully let go
of you

hunger thirst nourish

tears of pez

i don't let tears flow at will
i hold them deep down in my neck
until i'm alone
and then i spill
each
tear
one
by
one
tracking down my cheek
and lick each memory's sweet flavor
until the pain shuts my neck
with a creak

letting go

i wish it was
easy

ringing out
my tears

a kitchen sponge
drying out
on the counter

ready for
the next
dirty
dish

elle michelle

depression

when i woke up
my coffee was piping hot
now the sun is down
my coffee is cold and
my body hasn't moved
like the ice
i should have added
to my coffee

xanax

what's the point in living
without memories
you swallow pill after pill
just to get through the day
a day you forget about

you forget our
plans
you forget our
stories
i guess that means
the drugs
are working

you can't stress about a
life
you don't remember

the real thing

you grew
up on coke
chugging it
at 3 years-old
it's only natural
that you graduated
to the powdered stuff
at 23 we ignored it at first
chalking it up to your typical
sociopath behavior we didn't
know you were sprinkling the
demons inside you with turbo
pixie dust until you showed
up at our wedding blood
shot eyes stuffed in a
tuxedo your bow tie
couldn't hold back the
pressured speech and
disjointed thoughts our
bodies were dancing to
the music your body was
dancing to the seizure time
to face the problem the fairies
weren't coming to save you

bipolar

one second
waiting for water to boil
the next
bubbling over
ricocheting
between
extremes
never settling for a
simmer

elle michelle

man's first cry

no longer
held back
by his heart's
guarded chambers
he cried malt balls
tears so big
they made
plopping sounds
when they
hit
his shoes
and the
relief was

sweet

sweet

sweet

bitter sweet

i am cream and sugar
but also bitter coffee
you can't have one without the other
i've already been stirred together

elle michelle

stand out

i was the drop of

olive oil

in the pot of water
that refused to
act
like everyone else

hunger thirst nourish

pineapple perspective

some see a juicy fruit
while others see
tough, prickly skin
and wild hair

when life gives you lemons

if you place a single orange
into a sea of lemons
she will try to
hunch over
suck in her waist and
change her color
so she can morph into something
that resembles a lemon
unaware that
she
holds all the
sweetness
among a sea of sours

you sucked us dry

a maid of honor
is supposed to give a
champagne toast
at her best friend's wedding

instead
you let yourself
get drunk
with jealousy and resentment

too buzzed to see that you were
ruining our friendship
by toasting to
yourself
over and over and over

until there was no champagne left
to toast to our friendship

elle michelle

fake sweet

you gave me that kool aid smile
fake sweet
happy so happy
with my red cherry teeth

as long as i drank you
let your thoughts be my own
you were happy so happy
with your red cherry clone

you consumed all my glasses
my pitchers my cups
you were happy so happy
to be the one who filled me up

but when i took a sip of water
with which you did not agree
you were happy so happy
to disown me

i thought that i would miss
your fake sweet taste
but i was happy so happy
to have pure water in your place

insecurity hungers for
unsure thoughts
misinterpreted laughs
unrealistic comparisons

it will seduce you
it will lure you in
it will drain you
but
don't feed it
it will never be satisfied

find the sunlight
and stand in it
until it burns

vampires are not a myth

society has taught me to
dunk my cookies in
guilt
guilt for the calories
guilt for the lack of restraint
guilt for the preservatives
until all the enjoyment is
gone
i think it's time
to wash the guilt down
with a glass of milk

it does a psyche good

step one

i invited addiction in for a drink
i thought it a harmless date
but ever since he came over
i haven't been thinking straight

he slowly slipped into my mind
now he's an endless haunt
always talking in my head
telling me what i want

some nights are blacked out completely
there are dents and dings on my car
my family gives me worried looks
when i go out to the bar

i've been out every night
maybe it's too much
no one is happy when i'm home
so i don't see what's all the fuss

i've recently lost my job
i can't make it to work on time
addiction keeps telling me it's ok
but am i really fine

i thought addiction was my friend
now i'm starting to see
that i invited addiction in for a drink
and now he's drowning me

as i sit here at the bottom of the pool
filled with drinks addiction keeps mixing
i scream, the bubbles silently pop
i am powerless to this addiction

drinking
is a game
i play
with the
wilds
of my soul
who usually win

i let them

elle michelle

whiskey messy

some people like to drink whiskey neat
but when i drink whiskey
things
always
turn
messy

straight talk

give it to me straight
i can handle it
once things start getting muddled
i usually need a drink

still human

i wish i could distill my impurities
out into the air
i would take a hot shower
and boil them up through my hair

i could have a chance to start anew
fresh and free
until i make some more mistakes
and need another shower for impurity

the magic of rum

rum is transforming
have you seen what it can do
to
a
raisin

elle michelle

soul cirrhosis

right now
i need alcohol
to scar my liver
and poetry
to scar my soul

piping hot coffee

one sip
and i awoke
from my
groggy stupor
to realize
that we have
all burned
our mouths
it's whether
or not
we can
sip past
the pain

nourish

AND WHEN SHE

THE TOP BUTTON
OF HER
SOUL
SHE KNEW THAT SHE
HAD FILLED UP ON
THE RIGHT TYPE OF
NOURISHMENT

i've been
spilled
cracked and
broken
but
i've also been
clinked
chugged and
toasted

half empty or
half full
i realize that
i
am the cup
i
can fill it up
or empty it
at my
own will

preferably with champagne

elle michelle

one day i ate the sunset
plucked it straight from the sky
swallowed it down into my belly
as it burned my insides

and instead of exploding
i absorbed all the light
beaming from head to toe
i stood taller in my height

then when darkness came to visit
with his buddy mr. night
i was not scared or intimidated
for it was i who was

the light

you are not
insignificant
you are a
blow torch
just waiting
to caramelize
the world
with your flame

and everyone will stop and watch

elle michelle

bottomless

love yourself
endlessly
like a
bottomless buffet

every time
someone takes
go replenish
your tray

as long as you
keep making
self-love
it will never run out

it will overflow
on your plate
and that's when
you can give it out

double dip
into your heart
every day
love yourself
first and
second
and so on
forever

it starts and ends with you

coffee epiphany

and then she realized
that her favorite person
to have a cup of coffee with was
herself

i dance with all my
      wobbly
bits
      hanging
          out
i move my body to the
tune
of
the
music
while i
      undulate
          and
sway
      about
i don't care a bit
about who is looking
because i am in
my groove
i wish you would
come and join me
and move the way that

      jell-o
          moves

she wore her confidence
like a fluffernutter sandwich
as a perfectly
delicious
mess

and she knew it

exposed

lay it all out on the table
if they won't accept you
with all your seasonings
slivers and pieces
sprawled out to share
well then
more for you

perfection

the more i try to achieve it
the easier i collapse
i guess i'm more of a
rustic apple pie
than a perfectly puffed soufflé

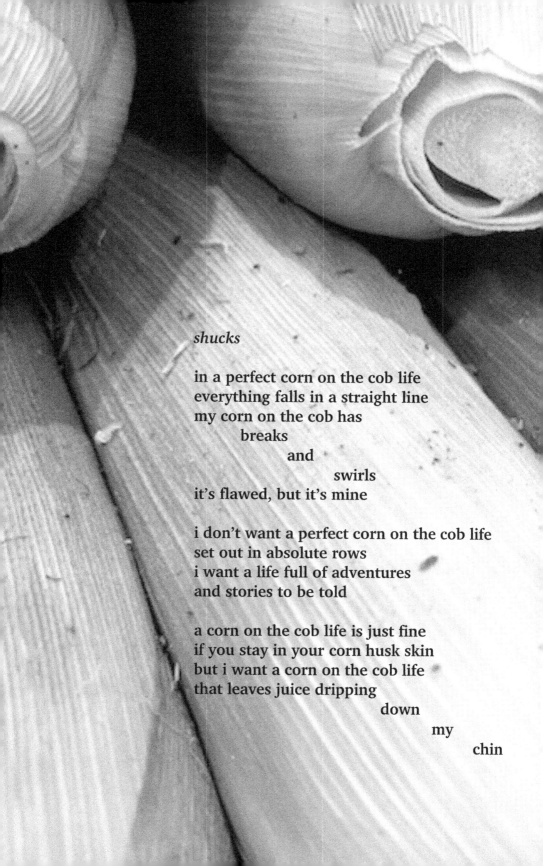

shucks

in a perfect corn on the cob life
everything falls in a straight line
my corn on the cob has
     breaks
         and
             swirls
it's flawed, but it's mine

i don't want a perfect corn on the cob life
set out in absolute rows
i want a life full of adventures
and stories to be told

a corn on the cob life is just fine
if you stay in your corn husk skin
but i want a corn on the cob life
that leaves juice dripping
             down
              my
               chin

we can learn from spaghetti
all slurpy and wet
loud and obnoxious
she has no regrets

she speaks her mind
stands up for what's right
she's not going in your mouth
without putting up a fight

she likes it even better
all covered in sauce
leave her mark on your face
no matter the cost

you won't forget spaghetti
she has the last word
speak up like spaghetti

let your voice be heard

just because I have manners
doesn't mean I don't know
how to dance on the table

i'll leave marks

elle michelle

scratch

i saw that my life was
flour
sugar
milk
and salt
and i could bake it
into anything i desired

hunger thirst nourish

you know that

pit

in your stomach
that is the seed of

growth

the lamb gets
just as hungry as
the wolf and
even though
the hunger
eats her up inside
she puts on a
calm and gentle face
because she would rather
starve
than become
the beast

self-control

elle michelle

regenerate

she is a beautiful
stone crab
without her largest claw
and while the world
focuses on her
brokenness
she focuses
on the healing
and the marvel of
growing back
into herself

sun dimples

why do i treat my cellulite as a dough
that i can mold
i've tried to roll it out
poke it down and
pound it into place
when i should be embracing
the womanly form that is uniquely me
proudly baking my dimples in the sun

stretch marks

i try to copy the snook
with her telling stripe
by displaying
the silvery stripes on my hips
in a proud fashion
fighting for them
aggressively
any time
someone tries to
reel
in my
self esteem

top
the cherry on

good enough for castration
good enough for sex with woman or man
good enough for selling
but not good enough for your own hand?

have we all forgotten that the clitoris
is a beautiful female part
yours and yours alone
to decide when you stop or start

don't be ashamed of your cherry
don't let unfound guilt consume
your precious female form
take control and let it bloom

.party

think about how women's lives would change
if we threw period parties every month
that celebrated with
yoga pants balloons
bloody bedsheets streamers and
red velvet cakes topped with
tampon candles
and ibuprofen sprinkles
and each woman left with the best party favor ever
the love for the miracle of her own womb

elle michelle

women   women
  supporting

now i know
i shouldn't compare
my pears to
your melons
i should be
lifting you up
to help you
support
the weight

girlfriends are like cosmopolitans
sometimes you sip them in slowly
sometimes you chug them down all at once
the more you drink them in
the more loose lipped and fun they become
until they are your

favorite drink

elle michelle

the best female bonding occurs
in the kitchen
with me stirring
and you chopping
and us talking
and laughing
with time disappearing in between
the smells
and sounds of

friendship cooking

hunger thirst nourish

mom

this squishy bosom
scratch pancake mixin' woman
planted my soul's roots

steeped tea

my father said
i've been steeping for awhile
i've experienced the
aromas
colors and
nuances
of life
but you,
you
are just starting to flavor
the water

elle michelle

burning advice

my dad always said
the best parts of the meat
are the burnt ends
for it's when you get
closest to the fire
that you can taste the
best parts of life

crust

i want to protect you
from the world
like crust over bread
but when you are ready and baked
i'll cut off the crust
and hope that i have given you
the best of the center

made with love

if we spread
our sandwiches
with love and humanity
the world would
never
go
hungry

dreamer

i am a gummy worm
inching through the dirt
wishing for crushed oreos

flavor: human

the world is made up of fruit stripe gum
each one of us a brightly different colored stripe
when you put a piece in the mouth of life
we all taste delightful and equally as nice

i've finally found
the sieve of
confidence
that drains my
d
o
u
b
t
s
but keeps
my heart

so i can follow it

the gold within

you were so unsuspecting
but when i unwrapped you
i found a golden ticket

elle michelle

you were the one
who came into my kitchen
and showed me how to bake
without a recipe
without measuring
just with an easy laugh and a

flour storm

pop rock feeling

the newness
crackles on my tongue
and pops on my heart
the tingling of a
fresh love
i wish for it
never to dissolve

elle michelle

sublimation

he could brew
laughter
out of
spent grain
and
dregs

hunger thirst nourish

apple picking

i thought all apples
were poisoned
until you showed me
an orchard

cereal milk

i hope our love soaks for awhile
in the milk of this life
so we can drink up
the sugary goodness
at the end

elle michelle

i'm your favorite dessert

i know that you love me
when you give me
the bigger half of chocolate cake
your favorite dessert
it tells me that you know
it doesn't matter how many bites of cake you eat
only that you eat them
while watching the one you love smile

the best for last

you are the
center
cinnamon roll
i
saved
for
last

all the fizzy ones

**i want to spend a million
champagne moments
with you**

cupcake

start by caressing
my frosting
with your fingers
swirling and flicking
tip of tongue licking
rhythmically clicking
until my frosting
melts
in
your
mouth

don't stop until
you've finished your meal
you have me
at the top of my cake
i don't have to fake
i only take
and take
and take
your aggressive bites
until
i crumble
into bits

sundae

when we make a sundae
we don't need ice cream
you scoop me right up
like a sexy dream

you cover me in sauce
lick me from head to toe
you melt me down to my core
as your head drops below

you take your time with my cherry
until i'm about to burst
then you split me wide open
until we both cry and curse

it's then i understand
the reason that they scream
you scream, i scream
we all scream for ice cream

there's no going back to bland

you were the salt
that woke up my taste buds
to the flavor of life
now i have to salt everything

béchamel

love is love
but a relationship is work
like making a béchamel sauce
butter, flour and then slowly
little by little
adding the milk
not too rushed
or the sauce will be lumpy
and not too slowly
or the sauce will burn
just right, taking your time
to mix and stir and add
just right and just so
until you have
the smoothest and the creamiest and
the most delicious sauce of your life
if you care for your relationship
like you care for a béchamel sauce
even though it is work and
even though it takes time and patience
it will be worth it because
a great love is always worth
every
last
saucy
bite

old love

i hope our love grows old
like the sucking candy
in my grandmother's purse
safe in a baggie
always a comfort
to each other
but also ready to be pulled out
and shared with those
who need to see
that a sweet love
can last

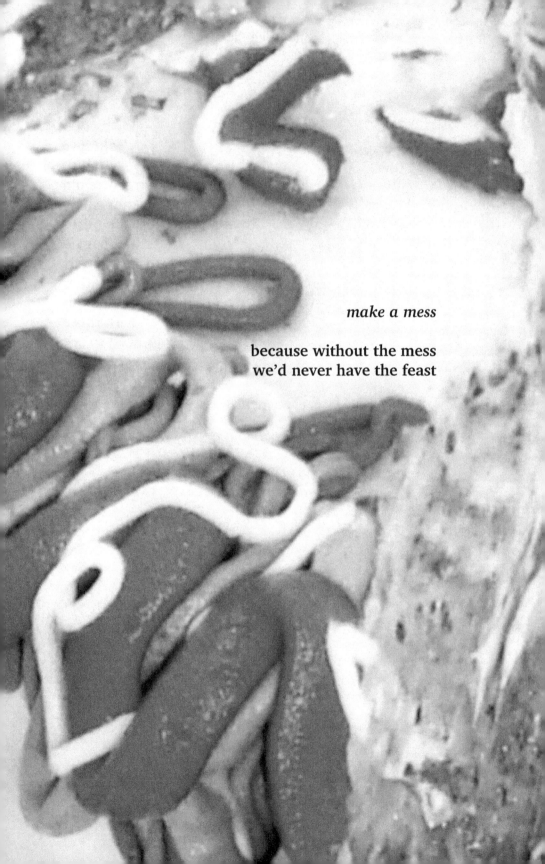

make a mess

because without the mess
we'd never have the feast

smash cake

don't feed me the wedding cake of life
in a clean and dainty fashion
sober
with the smallest piece on a fork
smash it all over my face
with your bare hands
and a champagne smirk

a biscuit
that crumbles
is normal

truth for us all

i forgive you

because i don't deserve
to carry around
leftovers
forever
and you deserve
a home cooked meal

elle michelle

to dine
is a rarity
most people
just eat

stop and smell this kitchen

at your table

you can set it
or keep it bare
you can eat
or starve
drink
or thirst
clear it
or leave it
just know that
whatever you choose
it will be
enough

evidence of living

life is short
leave lipstick stains
all over
shirt collars and
wine glasses

sow your seeds

i can only try
to grow
lead a fruitful life
and hope the seeds i planted
will blossom
more beautifully
and bear fruit
more plentifully
than me

elle michelle

the one and only

promise me
that one day
you will realize
that in this feast
you are a
delicacy

hunger thirst nourish

for my children

i hope you lick the bowl
i hope you get flour in your hair
and food in your teeth
i hope you wear milk mustaches
i hope you dance in the kitchen
and play with your peas
and i hope you eat dessert
lots and
lots
of dessert

elle michelle

give of yourself

be the
hot coffee
that warms
cold hands
you will find that
the generosity is
addictive

fork on the left

i hope that one day
we will sit at the
same table again
until then
i'll keep setting
your place

may i be excused

death will need to
roll me
out of this life
because I plan on
endlessly
feasting
drinking and
laughing
until my belly
aches with joy and
swells with
satisfaction

empty but full

i poured out the cup of
my mind
my heart and
my soul
to fill these pages for you
and as the pain spilled out
my cup did not empty
rather, it filled with gratitude
for you and the magic of poetry

about the book

the best story swaps
happen around the table
in this book
i am swapping stories
with you
i pass the stories of
my life
and the life of
my friends and family
along
to show you
that you are not
alone
we are all connected
through our story swaps
even bad beginnings
can often lead to
happy endings
if we let them
and i hope that one day
i will story swap with
you

about the author

elle michelle is a
native floridian
physician
wife
mother of three
lover of
food
drink
photography
travel
and florida living
who believes that
shared experiences
especially through
meals
is where the
essence
of life exists
and writing down
those experiences
poetically
can heal the pain
and spread the joy
of life and love